from SEA TO SHINING SEA
NEW JERSEY

By Dennis Brindell Fradin

CONSULTANTS

Abraham Resnick, Ed.D., Professor of Social Studies Education (Retired),
Jersey City State College

Robert L. Hillerich, Ph.D., Professor Emeritus, Bowling Green State University;
Consultant, Pinellas County Schools, Florida

CHILDRENS PRESS®
CHICAGO

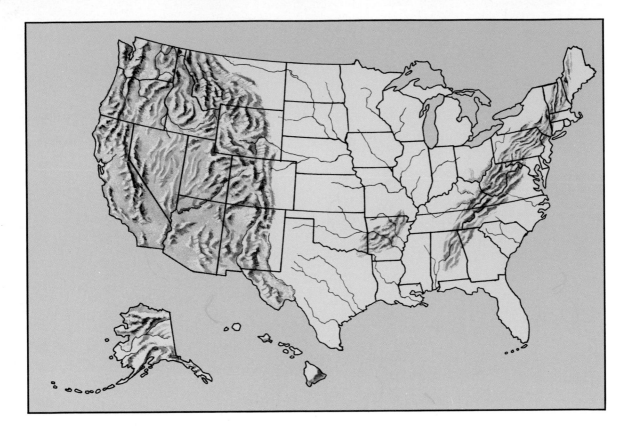

New Jersey is one of the three Middle Atlantic states. The other Middle Atlantic states are New York and Pennsylvania.

For April Burch

For his help, the author thanks Theodore Brunson, Director, Afro-American Historical Society Museum, Jersey City.

Project Editor: Joan Downing
Design Director: Karen Kohn
Research Assistant: Judith Bloom Fradin
Typesetting: Graphic Connections, Inc.
Engraving: Liberty Photoengraving

SECOND PRINTING, 1993.

Library of Congress Cataloging-in-Publication Data

Fradin, Dennis B.
  New Jersey / by Dennis Brindell Fradin.
   p.   cm. — (From sea to shining sea)
  Includes index.
  Summary: Introduces the geography, history, industries, notable sights, and famous people of the Garden State.
  ISBN 0-516-03830-3
  1. New Jersey—Juvenile literature. [1. New Jersey.]
I. Title. II. Series: Fradin, Dennis B. From sea to shining sea.
F134.3.F68   1993   92-34601
974.9—dc20   CIP
                                                AC

Table of Contents

Sailboats at Cape May

Introducing the Garden State

New Jersey is a small northeastern state along the Atlantic Ocean. It was named for England's Isle of Jersey. The state has long been known for its farms and gardens. New Jersey's nickname is the "Garden State."

New Jersey was one of England's thirteen American colonies. In 1775, the colonies rebelled against England. New Jersey became a battleground. George Washington won the battles of Trenton and Princeton there.

Today, New Jersey is a big producer of chemicals, packaged foods, and flowers. The state is also home to the Miss America Pageant. Each September, it is held in Atlantic City.

The Garden State is special in other ways. Where was the nation's first major dinosaur discovered? Where were the first baseball and college football games played? Where were President Grover Cleveland and author Judy Blume born? Where was the electric light invented? The answer to these questions is: New Jersey!

A picture map
of New Jersey

DUNNINGTON

The Seahorse-shaped State

THE SEAHORSE-SHAPED STATE

New Jersey's outline looks like a seahorse. This seahorse-shaped state has water on almost every side. The Delaware River forms its western border with Pennsylvania and Delaware. Delaware Bay is to the south. The Atlantic Ocean is to the east. The Hudson River separates northeastern New Jersey from New York. Its only waterless border is to the north with New York.

New Jersey is one of the three Middle Atlantic states. New York and Pennsylvania are the other two. New Jersey covers 7,787 square miles. Only four of the other forty-nine states are smaller. New Jersey could fit inside Alaska, the largest state, seventy-five times.

GEOGRAPHY

New Jersey's seaside beaches are its lowest points. The state's southern two-thirds is low, level coastland. Its northern third has hills and mountains. Most of the state's lakes are also in the north. Lake Hopatcong is New Jersey's largest lake. It covers

Sand patterns at Island Beach State Park

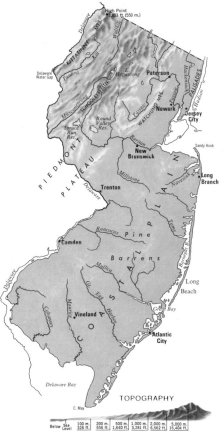

TOPOGRAPHY

| Below Sea Level | 100 m. 328 ft. | 200 m. 656 ft. | 500 m. 1,640 ft. | 1,000 m. 3,281 ft. | 2,000 m. 6,562 ft. | 5,000 m. 16,404 ft. |

only 4 square miles. New Jersey's tallest peak is near its northernmost tip. Called High Point, it rises 1,803 feet above sea level.

New Jersey is about 40 percent wooded. Northern New Jersey has oaks, maples, beeches, ashes, and pines. The red oak is the state tree. The purple violet grows in these woodlands. It is the state flower.

Oaks, cedars, and dwarf pines grow in the Pinelands. This is a large, marshy part of southern New Jersey. Dwarf pines stand only 5 feet tall when fully grown. Many kinds of orchids grow in the

Above left: Great Falls, on the Passaic River at Paterson
Below: Yellow lady's slippers grow in the Pinelands, which are also called the Pine Barrens.

Tree frogs like this live in the Pinelands.

The Kittatinny Mountains (left) and Buttermilk Falls (right) are in the Delaware Water Gap National Recreation Area.

Pinelands. So do pitcher plants. They trap and eat insects. The state's cranberries also grow in the Pinelands.

Deer run through New Jersey's woodlands. Foxes, raccoons, skunks, and opossums can also be seen. Bog lemmings live in the Pinelands. Snapping turtles hunt frogs there. Whales and dolphins swim offshore. The eastern goldfinch is the state bird. New Jersey's other birds include sea gulls, herons, and wild turkeys.

CLIMATE

New Jersey has a moderate climate. The ocean keeps the summers cool at the seashore. The state's

record high temperature, however, was 110 degrees Fahrenheit. This happened at Runyon on July 10, 1936.

The ocean also helps warm New Jersey's winters along the coastal areas. January temperatures often top 40 degrees Fahrenheit. But on January 5, 1904, the temperature fell to minus 34 degrees Fahrenheit. This is the state's record low. It happened at River Vale. The northern mountains are the state's snowiest area. They receive about 50 inches of snow per year. Southern New Jersey receives only about 13 inches of snow yearly.

Hurricanes sometimes strike New Jersey. They form over the ocean. Hurricane Hazel slammed into the state in 1954.

Winter scenes in Wharton State Forest (above) and at Wick Farm, near Morristown (below)

From Ancient Times Until Today

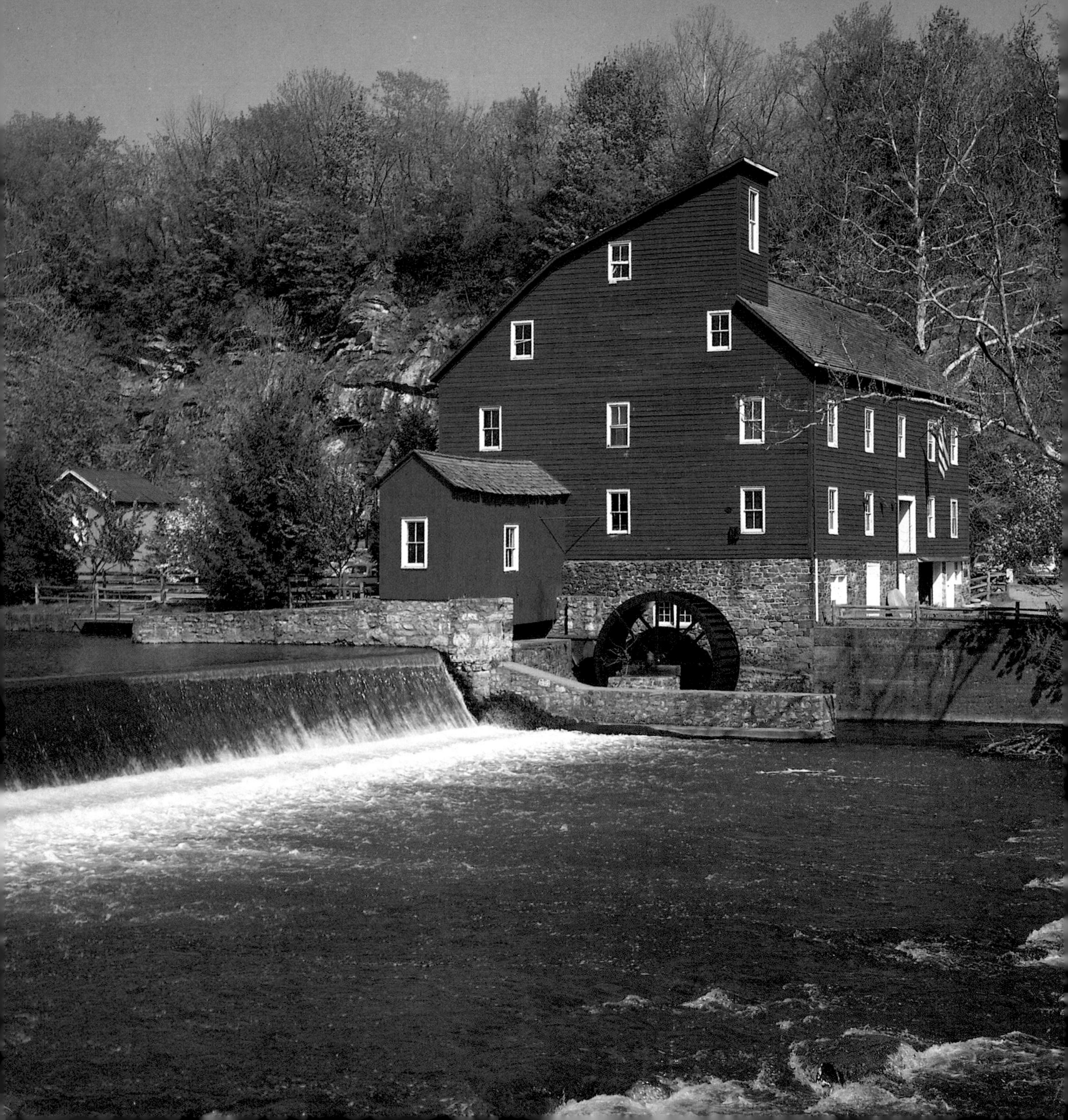

From Ancient Times Until Today

Hundreds of millions of years ago, dinosaurs roamed across New Jersey. In 1858, dinosaur bones were discovered at Haddonfield. That dinosaur was named Hadrasaurus. It was 30 feet long. It had a bill like a duck's. Hadrasaurus was the first dinosaur found in the United States.

About 2 million years ago, the Ice Age began. About 20,000 years ago, glaciers covered northern New Jersey. These huge ice sheets dug deep holes. The holes filled with water and became lakes. Ice also carved the Palisades. These are cliffs along the Hudson River.

American Indians

Ancient Indians reached New Jersey about 10,000 years ago. These early New Jerseyans hunted and fished. About 1,000 years ago, American Indians learned to farm. They settled in villages where they grew crops.

In later times, New Jersey was home to Lenni-Lenape Indians. They lived in dome-shaped houses

A Lenape Indian village has been recreated at Waterloo, in Morristown National Historical Park. The stone tools, baskets, and pottery bowls in the picture below were modeled after those that were used by the Lenape. The Lenape were part of the Algonquian group of Indians.

called wigwams. The women grew corn, beans, and squash. The men hunted deer and bears with bows and arrows.

The Lenni-Lenape were a peaceful people. They gave food to strangers who stopped at their villages. They even settled other tribes' disputes. Out of respect, other tribes called them "Our Grandparents."

EXPLORERS

Giovanni da Verrazano was the first known explorer in New Jersey. He was an Italian sailing for France. Verrazano explored New Jersey's northern shore in 1524. But France did not settle this land.

In 1609, Henry Hudson sailed up the Hudson River in his ship, the Half Moon.

Henry Hudson arrived in 1609. This famous English explorer worked for the Netherlands. Hudson sailed up the river that was later named for him. Because of his voyage, the Netherlands claimed a piece of North America. They called it New Netherland. It contained parts of five present-day states. They are New York, New Jersey, Delaware, Connecticut, and Pennsylvania.

Explorer Henry Hudson

DUTCH AND SWEDISH SETTLERS

Dutch settlers came from the Netherlands. In 1630, they founded Pavonia. It was across the Hudson River from New York City. Some Dutch traders set up posts along Delaware Bay.

Sweden, too, claimed a piece of North America. It was called New Sweden. New Sweden contained parts of New Jersey, Delaware, and Pennsylvania. In 1638, a few Swedish people settled in southern New Jersey.

Both the Dutch and the Swedish were fur traders. In 1655, the Dutch took over New Sweden. In 1660, they began New Jersey's first permanent non-Indian town. This was Bergen. It is now part of Jersey City. By 1663, only about 200 colonists lived in New Jersey.

England Rules New Jersey

By 1630, England had colonies in New England, Virginia, and the Carolinas. In 1664, an English fleet captured New Jersey. The English gave New Jersey its name. They founded new towns, including Elizabeth and Newark. Under English rule, people poured into New Jersey. They came from Europe and from other colonies. Quakers settled Burlington in West New Jersey in 1677. It became the capital. In 1686, Perth Amboy in East New Jersey also became a capital.

By 1760, New Jersey had about 100,000 settlers and 100 towns. The towns became trading centers. Factories were built. Glassmaking, cloth making, and shipbuilding became important New Jersey businesses.

New Jersey's colonists grew wheat and corn. They raised hogs, cows, and chickens. New Jersey's farms earned the colony a nickname. It was "Garden of North America." Later, New Jersey became known as the Garden State.

Schools opened for young New Jerseyans. Two universities were begun. Princeton was founded in 1746. Rutgers started in 1766. Of England's colonies, only New Jersey had two colleges.

From 1686 to 1790, New Jersey had two capitals at the same time. Until 1702, New Jersey had two parts: West New Jersey and East New Jersey.

Rutgers University (above) was founded in 1766.

THE REVOLUTIONARY WAR

In the 1760s, England began taxing the Americans more heavily. The colonists rebelled. In late 1774, New Jerseyans burned English tea at Greenwich. This "Greenwich Tea Party" protested the tax on tea.

America's dispute with England got worse. It led to the Revolutionary War (1775-1783). About 20,000 New Jerseyans fought for America's freedom. Several New Jerseyans led America's fight for

The Revolutionary War Battle of Monmouth (above) was fought on June 28, 1778.

Massachusetts' colonists held the more famous Boston Tea Party.

17

Above: Molly Pitcher at the Battle of Monmouth.
Below: Muskets being fired at a Princeton Battle reenactment

freedom. William Livingston was New Jersey's wartime governor. He escaped many British attempts to capture or kill him. Reverend John Witherspoon was a minister. He was the only minister to sign the Declaration of Independence. This was the paper that created the United States.

New Jersey became known as the "Cockpit of the Revolution." Three major battles were fought there. George Washington's army won the Battle of Trenton on December 26, 1776. It also won the Battle of Princeton on January 3, 1777. The Battle of Monmouth was fought on June 28, 1778. That was a hot day. Mary Ludwig Hays brought pitchers

of water to Washington's men. The soldiers called her "Molly Pitcher." Hays even helped fire a cannon during the battle.

The battle of Monmouth ended in a draw. Five years later, the Americans won the war. The thirteen colonies had become the United States of America.

GROWTH OF THE THIRD STATE

In 1787, American leaders wrote the United States Constitution. This was a strong framework of government. New Jersey signed the Constitution on December 18, 1787. On that day, New Jersey became the third state. William Livingston was New Jersey's first state governor. Trenton became the state capital in 1790.

New cities and industries grew in the third state. Paterson was founded in 1791. It became a cloth-making center. In Hoboken, John Stevens built steamboats. In 1809, his *Phoenix* traveled out to sea. It became the first steamboat ever to do this. In 1825, Stevens built the country's first steam locomotive. Stevens's locomotive chugged along at 12 miles an hour. That's slower than a person can run.

Paterson then became a center for making locomotives. Between 1837 and about 1880, about

William Livingston, New Jersey's first state governor

Below: A sketch of the first locomotive built in America

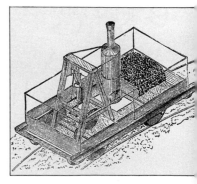

19

6,000 of them were made there. Those locomotives were shipped all across North and South America.

Trains, ships, and stagecoaches brought more people to New Jersey. From 1800 to 1850, the population rose from 211,149 to 489,555 people.

The growing state was the site of two sports "firsts." The first baseball game was played in Hoboken on June 19, 1846. The New York Nine beat the Knickerbocker Baseball Club 23-1. The first college football game was played on November 6, 1869. In New Brunswick, Rutgers beat Princeton on that long-ago Saturday. The score was 6-4.

SLAVERY AND THE CIVIL WAR

At one time, all thirteen colonies had allowed slavery. In 1784, New Jerseyans owned about 2,000 slaves. In 1804, New Jersey passed a law to free its slaves. The other northern states also ended slavery. The South continued to allow slavery.

Quakers and other New Jerseyans helped southern slaves escape. They were part of the Underground Railroad. This was a series of hiding places. Slaves used them when escaping to Canada. William Still was a black writer. He turned his home outside Camden into an Underground Railroad sta-

Below: A re-creation of a Civil War camp at New Bridge Landing, New Milford

tion. Sarah and Angelina Grimké's home was also a major station. The Grimké sisters lived in Perth Amboy. They wrote and spoke against slavery.

In 1861, the North and the South began fighting. This was called the Civil War (1861-1865). It was fought over slavery and other issues. No battles were fought in New Jersey. But more than 88,000 New Jerseyans fought for the North. The country's remaining slaves were freed by the North's victory.

NEW JERSEY INVENTIONS AND PRESIDENTS

By the late 1800s, New Jersey was a great industrial state. New Jersey's cities made cloth, jewelry, and shoes. They also made pottery, bricks, and machinery. Thousands of people came from Ireland, Germany, and Italy. They worked in New Jersey's factories.

Thomas Edison worked in Menlo Park, New Jersey. The "Wizard of Menlo Park" invented the record player in 1877. Two years later, he invented the electric light. During the 1880s, Edison helped invent moving pictures—the movies. One movie showed a man sneezing. Others showed circus acts and people dancing. Fort Lee, New Jersey, was the country's first movie capital. The first film that told

In 1887, Thomas Edison (below) moved from Menlo Park to laboratories in West Orange (above).

Later, Hollywood, California, became the country's movie center.

a story was made there in 1903. Its title was *The Great Train Robbery.*

Two New Jerseyans served as president about this time. New Jersey-born Grover Cleveland was the twenty-second president (1885-1889). Cleveland was also the twenty-fourth president (1893-1897). He was the only president to serve two terms that weren't back-to-back. Woodrow Wilson was the twenty-eighth president (1913-1921). He was born in Virginia. Wilson served as Princeton University's president (1902-1910). Then he served as New Jersey's governor (1911-1913).

Woodrow Wilson

WORLD WARS AND DEPRESSION

Wilson was president when the country entered World War I (1914-1918) in 1917. About 130,000 New Jersey soldiers and sailors helped win the war. The state also made ships, airplanes, and weapons for the war effort.

Hard times known as the Great Depression (1929-1939) struck the country. Factories closed. Many New Jerseyans lost their jobs. Thousands of New Jerseyans waited in breadlines for food.

World War II (1939-1945) helped end the Great Depression. The United States entered this war in 1941. New Jersey's factories swung into action. Once again, they made much-needed weapons, ships, and uniforms. More than 560,000 New Jerseyans served in uniform.

RECENT DEVELOPMENTS AND PROBLEMS

In 1948, the transistor was invented in New Jersey. John Bardeen, Walter Brattain, and William Shockley invented it at Bell Laboratories. Transistors are used in radios, computers, and televisions.

Today, satellites beam television shows from one country to another. They also send weather reports

Many New Jerseyans lost their jobs during the Great Depression.

back to earth. *Tiros I* was the first satellite to take good weather pictures. It was launched in 1960. *Telstar I* was the first satellite to beam television shows between the United States and Europe. It was launched in 1962. Both satellites were developed in New Jersey.

Down on the ground, though, New Jersey had problems. Many black New Jerseyans were kept from good jobs and good housing. In 1967, black neighborhoods in several New Jersey cities had riots. The bloodiest riot was in Newark. About twenty-six people were killed there. Another 1,000 were hurt. In 1970, Kenneth A. Gibson was elected mayor of Newark. He was the city's first black mayor. Gibson worked to improve life for Newark's poor people.

Tourism has boomed throughout New Jersey in recent years. In 1976, New Jersey passed a law to allow gambling casinos in Atlantic City. New hotels with gambling casinos were built there. In 1985, about 30 million people visited the city. That made Atlantic City the country's top tourist resort. By the 1990s, New Jersey had nearly 20 million overnight visitors each year.

In 1987, the Garden State celebrated its 200th birthday. New Jersey, like many other parts of the

country, began its third century of statehood facing big problems. Urban areas have been especially hard hit. In 1992, one adult in ten was out of work. Parts of older New Jersey cities were deteriorating. Two-thirds of Camden's children lived in poverty. One-third of Newark's people were poor. Water and air pollution were high.

New Jerseyans are dealing with these problems. They have taken steps to help poor New Jerseyites. Parts of Newark, Jersey City, and Trenton have been rebuilt. There are plans to improve the schools and fight pollution. In 1879, an inventor working in New Jersey gave the world the electric light. Perhaps others will find ways to improve life in America's cities.

Atlantic City, with its Boardwalk, beaches, hotels, and gambling casinos, draws millions of tourists each year.

25

New Jerseyans and Their Work

New Jerseyans and Their Work

The 1990 Census counted 7,748,634 New Jerseyans. Only eight states have more people. New Jersey has about 995 people per square mile. It is the most crowded of the fifty states. Most New Jerseyans live in cities.

New Jerseyans come from all parts of the world. About 1 million New Jerseyans are black. Nearly 775,000 are Hispanic. Almost 272,000 New Jerseyans trace their roots to Asia. Many white New Jerseyans have Dutch, Swedish, English, Irish, and German backgrounds. The families of over 2 million New Jerseyans came from Italy.

New Jersey is home to people from all parts of the world and many ethnic backgrounds.

Their Work

Another of New Jersey's nicknames is the "Workshop of the Nation." New Jersey is one of the top ten manufacturing states. More than 650,000 of New Jersey's 4 million workers make products.

Chemicals are the state's top product. Only Texas leads New Jersey at making chemicals. New Jersey ranks number one at making medicines. It also ranks first at making soaps and cleaners.

These boys joined the work force at an early age. They are selling produce from their grandmother's farm.

Foods are New Jersey's second-leading product. The Garden State is among the top ten food-packaging states. Many canned and frozen fruits and vegetables come from New Jersey. The state also ranks high at making books, plastics, computers, and machinery.

More than 1 million New Jerseyans are service workers. Many of them work in hotels, restaurants, and resorts. Many others are health-care workers. Another million New Jerseyans sell goods. The state is home to 550,000 government workers. About 140,000 scientists and engineers live in New Jersey. More than 240,000 New Jerseyans work in real estate and insurance. Prudential is based in Newark. It is the country's biggest life insurance company.

The Garden State is home to about 40,000 farmers. Orchids, roses, and other flowers are top farm money-makers. Nursery products such as ornamental shrubs also rank high. New Jersey also grows blueberries, cranberries, peaches, and lettuce. Tomatoes, snap beans, sweet corn, asparagus, peppers, and eggplants are other vegetables. Milk and eggs are other major farm products.

A few hundred New Jerseyans fish for a living. The state has huge clam beds. Other shellfish caught include lobsters and oysters. Fish include flounder, menhaden, and sea bass.

New Jersey has only about 2,500 miners. The state's main minerals are stone, granite, and sand and gravel.

This New Jerseyan makes a living as a firefighter.

A Trip Through
the Garden State

A Trip Through the Garden State

No other state packs as much variety into so little space. New Jersey has big cities and small towns. It has farms, woods, mountains, and beaches. All these things are in a state one-twentieth the size of California.

The twin towers of New York City's World Trade Center can be seen from Jersey City.

Northeastern New Jersey

Northeastern New Jersey has the largest number of the state's people. Thousands of New Jerseyans cross the Hudson River to work in nearby New York City. The Holland and Lincoln tunnels help some of them get to work. Others use bridges.

Most of New Jersey's big cities are in the northeast. They include the state's four largest cities: Newark, Jersey City, Paterson, and Elizabeth.

Newark is a good place to start a New Jersey tour. It was settled in 1666. Newark is one of the country's oldest major cities. Newark is also New Jersey's largest city. The city is a banking, life insurance, and chemical-making center.

The New Jersey Symphony and State Opera are based in Newark. The Newark Museum has art-

works from around the world. American Indian objects are also displayed there. A one-room school dating from 1784 stands on the museum's grounds. The New Jersey Historical Society in Newark has a Kid's Center. Life in New Jersey in 1750, 1850, and 1950 is shown. Children may dress in clothing from those times.

The Newark skyline and the Passaic River

Jersey City is a few miles east of Newark. The Dutch founded it as Bergen in 1660. The English later named the town Jersey City. It is the state's second-biggest city.

The Old Bergen Church is a Jersey City landmark. It dates from the 1840s. Jersey City also has one of the world's largest clocks. It is called the Colgate Clock. The minute hand is 26 feet long.

Liberty State Park (above) is just one-fourth of a mile from the Statue of Liberty.

The Giants and Jets have "New York" in their names because they started in New York City.

Paterson was named for William Paterson, a New Jersey signer of the United States Constitution.

The Afro-American Historical Society Museum is another Jersey City highlight. There, visitors can learn much about black New Jerseyans.

Jersey City people think another landmark should be theirs, too. The Statue of Liberty is in New York Bay. It is on New Jersey's side of the bay. But New York was granted Liberty Island in 1833. That's where the statue stands. This is why the statue is considered part of New York.

Jersey City owns Liberty State Park. From there, visitors can take a ferry to the statue. The Liberty Science Center opened in the park in 1993. This museum has displays on inventions and health. It also has an eight-story-tall model of a tornado.

A few miles northwest is Lyndhurst. Its Trash Museum shows how recycling can stop pollution. A few miles farther north is East Rutherford. The Meadowlands Sports Complex is there. The New York Giants and the New York Jets play football at the Meadowlands. The New York Nets play basketball there. The center is also home to the New Jersey Devils. That's the pro hockey team.

Paterson is north of the Meadowlands. Alexander Hamilton founded Paterson in 1791. It was the country's first planned manufacturing city. In 1836, Samuel Colt began making guns there.

34

They were called Colt revolvers. Locomotives and silk were other early Paterson products. The Paterson Museum traces the city's business roots.

Paterson is now the state's third-largest city. It is still a manufacturing leader. Chemicals and many other goods are made there.

New Jersey's oldest English town is Elizabeth. It is just southwest of Newark. The town was begun in 1664. It was named for Elizabeth Carteret. She was the wife of a big New Jersey landowner. Today, Elizabeth is the Garden State's fourth-largest city.

Boxwood Hall in Elizabeth was home to Elias Boudinot. He was a president of the country's Revolutionary War government. George

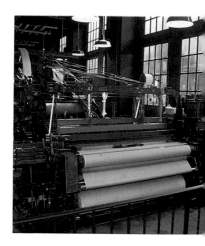

Among the exhibits at the Paterson Museum are this textile loom (above) and a locomotive built in 1909 (below).

This bust of Thomas Edison can be seen at the Edison National Historic Site.

Grover Cleveland's birthplace (below) is in Caldwell.

Washington stayed there in 1789. He was on his way to New York to become president.

The country's greatest inventor lived in northeastern New Jersey. The Thomas Edison National Historic Site is at West Orange. Edison's home, Glenmont, is there. The Thomas Edison Memorial Tower and Museum is at Menlo Park. Edison invented the electric light on this spot.

The Grover Cleveland Birthplace is near West Orange at Caldwell. Visitors can see the president's baby cradle. A piece of fruitcake is also on display. It is from his White House wedding in 1886. Cleveland was the only president to get married in the White House.

THE NEW JERSEY COAST

The New Jersey coast begins in the north around Sandy Hook. This hook-shaped sandy land stretches into the ocean. The Sandy Hook Lighthouse light first went on in 1764. The lighthouse has been used ever since. It has had the longest use of any lighthouse in the country.

Long Branch is just down the coast from Sandy Hook. This town was once a favorite vacation spot of United States presidents. It was even nicknamed

the country's "summer capital." President James Garfield asked to be taken to Long Branch after he was shot in Washington, D. C. Garfield died in Long Branch on September 19, 1881.

Islands belonging to New Jersey lie just off the mainland. Ship Bottom is a resort town on Long Beach Island. It is said that a ship landed there, upside down. Tapping came from inside the ship's bottom. A hole was chopped. Out stepped a girl who had survived the wreck. Barnegat Lighthouse is also on Long Beach Island. "Old Barney" dates back to 1858.

South of Long Beach Island are several small islands. They are part of Brigantine National Wildlife Refuge. Water birds nest in its wetlands.

Left: St. Michael's Church, in Long Branch
Right: Barnegat Lighthouse, on Long Beach Island

37

The beach at Atlantic City

Cape May diamonds

To the south is Absecon Island. Atlantic City, America's most popular resort, is there. About 32 million people visit Atlantic City each year. The whole state of New Jersey has less than one-fourth that many people.

Atlantic City's Boardwalk stretches along the beach. It was the country's first above-ground wooden walkway. Hotels, shops, and restaurants line this famous walk. Miss America hopefuls walk along the Boardwalk each September.

Anyone who has played Monopoly knows about the Boardwalk. Charles Darrow came up with this game in 1930. This was during the depression. Darrow, a salesperson, didn't have a job. He named the Monopoly streets after those in Atlantic City. It was his favorite vacation spot. There's a plaque at the corner of Park Place and the Boardwalk. It honors Darrow.

Cape May is at New Jersey's southeastern tip. It's the country's oldest seaside resort town. More than 600 homes date from the 1800s. Visitors find "Cape May diamonds" on the beaches. They are pieces of quartz—not real diamonds. People make rings, necklaces, and bracelets with them.

Visitors also come to Cape May to see wildlife. The Cape May Whale Watch and Research Center offers boat tours. On the tours, people watch for whales and dolphins. Each fall, teams of bird-watchers come to Cape May. They take part in the "World Series of Birding." For twenty-four hours, they look for different kinds of water birds. There are more than 700 different kinds. The team that spots the most kinds is the winner.

North of Cape May is the town of Wildwood. It's on an island. Each June, this town hosts the National Marbles Tournament. Children ages eight to fourteen win prizes for shooting marbles.

The Abbey is a beautifully painted Victorian seaside inn in Cape May.

Left: A Pine Barrens cranberry bog
Right: The general store and post office in Batsto Village

THE SOUTHERN INTERIOR

The Pinelands are in southeastern New Jersey. Early Pineland inhabitants farmed, hunted, and picked wild cranberries and blueberries. Many were fine woodworkers. Today, many Pineland people work in the region's cranberry bogs.

Batsto is in the northern Pinelands. It was an iron-making town during the Revolutionary War. Cannonballs for George Washington's army were made there. A village of the early 1800s has been rebuilt.

Southwest of Batsto is Millville. It is home to the country's largest museum of American glass-making. This is the Museum of American Glass.

Glass objects dating back to colonial times can be seen. Visitors can also watch glass being made.

Northwest of Millville is Bridgeton. There, visitors can learn much about New Jersey's Indians. The Woodruff Indian Museum has about 20,000 Lenni-Lenape tools, pipes, and clay pots. A Lenni-Lenape village has been rebuilt there. Present-day Lenni-Lenapes hold a powwow in Bridgeton each June.

North of Bridgeton is Glassboro. It was named for its many glassmaking factories. In June 1967, Glassboro became well known. President Lyndon Johnson and Aleksei Kosygin had a meeting there. Kosygin was the Soviet Union's leader.

Northwest of Glassboro is Gibbstown. The country's oldest-known log cabin is there. It's called Nothnagle Log House. Swedish settlers built it about 1640.

CITIES ON THE DELAWARE: CAMDEN AND TRENTON

Camden is in southwest New Jersey. The city lies across the Delaware River from Philadelphia, Pennsylvania. Camden was settled in 1681. Today, Camden is New Jersey's sixth-largest city.

Seals at the New Jersey State Aquarium, in Camden

The Old Barracks, in Trenton

Poet Walt Whitman (1819-1892) spent his last nineteen years in Camden. Whitman liked to talk to people—even strangers—on Camden's streets. Today, people can visit the Walt Whitman House. It is a Camden landmark.

Campbell Soup is based in Camden. The company has its own museum. The Campbell Museum has soup bowls dating back 2,500 years. In 1992, the New Jersey State Aquarium opened. The seals and sharks make a big splash with children.

Trenton lies on the Delaware River. It is halfway up New Jersey's western border. The town was begun in 1679. It was named for William Trent. He was a merchant who helped the young town grow. The William Trent House is the city's oldest house. It was built in 1719.

Trenton has been New Jersey's capital since 1790. New Jersey lawmakers meet in the state capitol. The building has a golden dome.

The New Jersey State Museum is in Trenton. Dinosaur fossils and Indian relics are displayed there. The Old Barracks Museum has guns, clothing, and furniture that date from 1759 to 1783. Both English and American soldiers stayed there. But not at the same time. In 1776, George Washington won the Battle of Trenton near there.

THE NORTHERN INTERIOR

Princeton is northeast of Trenton. It is home to Princeton University. Presidents James Madison and Woodrow Wilson went to Princeton. Nassau Hall is a well-known university building. In 1777, the Battle of Princeton ended at the hall. American cannon fire forced English troops to surrender. Nassau Hall served as the country's capitol in 1783. At that time, Princeton was the United States capital.

Left: The New Jersey state capitol was built in 1795.
Right: Blair Hall, at Princeton University

North of Princeton is Morristown. Nearby is Morristown National Historical Park. There, the huts in which Washington's men passed the winter of 1779-80 have been rebuilt. Ford House served as Washington's headquarters that winter. Martha Washington stayed there with him.

Northwest of Morristown is Stanhope. Washington would feel at home at Stanhope. An entire village of the 1700s has been rebuilt there. It is called Waterloo Village.

Northwestern New Jersey has many scenic spots. Delaware Water Gap is near Columbia at the

Rebuilt Revolutionary War soldiers' quarters (above) and the Wick Farm (below) are on the property of Morristown National Historical Park.

Pennsylvania border. Here, the Delaware River carved through the Kittatinny Mountains. This happened millions of years ago. The walls above the river are one-fourth of a mile high.

High Point is a good place to end a New Jersey tour. It is in the Kittatinny Mountains. High Point is the state's tallest peak. New Jersey, New York, and Pennsylvania meet there. Visitors enjoy the view of the three states from there. The New Jersey War Memorial is at High Point. It honors New Jerseyans who died in the country's wars.

Above: This statue of General George Washington can be seen at Morristown National Historical Park.
Below: High Point, in the Kittatinny Mountains

A Gallery of Famous New Jerseyans

A Gallery of Famous New Jerseyans

The Garden State has produced many great people. Many of the country's leaders have come from New Jersey. New Jerseyans also include writers, actors, and athletes.

John Woolman (1720-1772) was born near Rancocas. He was a Quaker. Woolman was one of early America's strongest enemies of slavery. In 1754, he wrote an antislavery pamphlet.

Patience Lovell Wright (1725-1786) was born in New York. But she grew up in Bordentown. Wright became one of America's first great sculptors. Her statue of William Pitt is in Westminster Abbey. That is a well-known church in London, England. Pitt was an English government leader.

Alexander Hamilton (1755-1804) was a New Yorker. He was the first U.S. secretary of the treasury (1789-1795). He founded Paterson, New Jersey, in 1791. **Aaron Burr** (1756-1836) was born in Newark. He was the country's vice president from 1801 to 1805. Burr and Hamilton were bitter enemies. They fought a duel at Weehawken, New Jersey on July 11, 1804. Hamilton was shot. He died the next day. In 1807, Burr was accused of try-

James Fenimore Cooper

Stephen Crane

ing to set up another country. He owned land around Louisiana. Burr spent his last years a lonely man.

Francis Hopkinson (1737-1791) was born in Pennsylvania. He later moved to Bordentown. There, he became a government leader. Hopkinson signed the Declaration of Independence in 1776. He designed the Great Seal of the United States. He also designed the first Stars and Stripes, the U.S. flag. Hopkinson wrote "My Days Have Been So Wondrous Free." It was one of the first nonreligious songs written in America.

Zebulon Pike (1779-1813) was born in what is now Trenton. He became a soldier and explorer. In 1806, he discovered a mountain peak in Colorado. It was named Pikes Peak for him.

The Garden State has produced many great authors. **James Fenimore Cooper** (1789-1851) was born in Burlington. He became a well-known author. Cooper wrote *The Last of the Mohicans.*

Stephen Crane (1871-1900) was another famous author. He was born in Newark. Crane wrote *The Red Badge of Courage.* This is a novel about the Civil War. Newark was also the birthplace of **Albert Payson Terhune** (1872-1942). Terhune wrote beautiful stories about dogs. *Lad: A Dog* and *The Heart of a Dog* are two of them.

William Carlos Williams (1883-1963) was born in Rutherford. He became a great poet. His poem *Paterson* is about that New Jersey City. He won the Pulitzer Prize for poetry in 1963. Williams was also a doctor. He cared for the children of Rutherford for about fifty years.

Joyce Kilmer (1886-1918) was born in New Brunswick. In 1913, he published a poem called "Trees." It is perhaps the best-known poem by an American. Kilmer was killed in World War I. He was only thirty-one.

Joyce Kilmer

Each year the Newbery Medal is awarded to a children's book author. **Joseph Krumgold** (1908-1980) won two Newbery Medals. He was the first author to do that. Krumgold was born in Jersey City. He won the 1954 Newbery for . . . *And Now Miguel.* He won again in 1960 for *Onion John.* **William Pène du Bois** was born in Nutley in 1916. He won the 1948 Newbery for *The Twenty-One Balloons.*

Judy Blume was born in Elizabeth in 1938. Her first major book was *Are You There, God? Its Me, Margaret.* Later works include *Tales of a Fourth Grade Nothing, Deenie,* and *Blubber.* Millions of young people have read these books. They feel that no one understands them as well as Blume.

Alice Paul

Sarah Vaughan

Charles Addams (1912-1988) was born in Westfield. As a child, he drew pictures of skulls and bones. Addams became a cartoonist. He drew a strange family of monsters. The television show "The Addams Family" was based on his drawings. Later, the movie *The Addams Family* was made.

Alice Paul (1885-1977) was born in Moorestown. She fought for women's right to vote. Her work helped women win the vote in 1920.

Many great entertainers came from the Garden State. **Paul Robeson** (1898-1976) was born in Princeton. He earned top grades at Rutgers. He also starred in football there. Then Robeson earned a law degree at Columbia in New York. Later, Robeson became a great actor and singer. *Show Boat* was one of his best-loved films.

Two all-time jazz greats were New Jerseyans. Pianist and band leader **William "Count" Basie** (1904-1984) was born in Red Bank. Singer **Sarah Vaughan** (1924-1990) was born in Newark. **Frank Sinatra** is one of America's most popular singers. He was born in Hoboken in 1915. People call him "Old Blue Eyes." **Dionne Warwick** (born in Orange in 1940), **Paul Simon** (born in Newark in 1942), and **Bruce Springsteen** (born in Freehold in 1949) also won fame as singers.

Abbott and Costello made millions of people laugh. They played on radio, television, and the stage. They also made movies. **Bud Abbott** (1896-1974) was born in Asbury Park. **Lou Costello** (1908-1959) was born in Paterson. Their best-known routine is "Who's on First?"

Jack Nicholson was born in Neptune in 1937. He played the Joker in the movie *Batman*. Nicholson has won Academy Awards for roles in two other films. Actress **Meryl Streep** was born in Summit in 1949. She has also won two Academy Awards. Streep won an Emmy for her role in "Holocaust." **John Travolta** was born in Englewood in 1954. He was a star in the television show "Welcome Back, Kotter." He also starred in the movie *Look Who's Talking*.

Meryl Streep

Left: Paul Simon
Right: Count Basie

Bill Bradley (above) once scored 58 points in a game at Princeton. That's still a school record.

Franco Harris

Amos Alonzo Stagg (1862-1965) was born in West Orange. He was a great football coach. Stagg retired at the age of eighty-four. He had 314 victories. The "Grand Old Man of Football" lived to be 102.

William "Bill" Bradley was born in Missouri in 1943. He was a top student at Princeton University (1960-1965). He also starred in basketball there. He played for the New York Knicks (1967-1977). Bradley has since served New Jersey as a U.S. senator (1979-present). Football great **Franco Harris** was born at Fort Dix in 1950. He scored 100 touchdowns as a pro.

Track star **Carl Lewis** was born in Alabama in 1961. He grew up in Willingboro, New Jersey. Lewis won a total of eight Olympic gold medals. He won them at the 1984, 1988, and 1992 Olympics. In 1991, he set a world record in the 100-meter dash. He ran it in 9.86 seconds.

Edwin "Buzz" Aldrin went faster and farther than even Carl Lewis. Aldrin was born in Montclair in 1930. He became an astronaut. In July 1969, he became the second person to walk on the moon.

Virginia Apgar (1909-1974) made up the first test that children take. She was born in Westfield. Apgar was a doctor. She helped in the births of

more than 17,000 babies. In 1952, Apgar created the Apgar Score. It measures a baby's health at birth. Most babies score near a perfect ten. Babies with low Apgar Scores need extra help.

Left: Edwin Aldrin
Right: Carl Lewis

Home to Dr. Virginia Apgar, Abbott and Costello, Patience Lovell Wright, Paul Robeson, and Judy Blume . . .

Site of the battles of Trenton, Princeton, and Monmouth . . .

The state where the electric light and movies were developed . . .

A leader at producing chemicals, packaged foods, clothing, blueberries, and lettuce . . .

This is New Jersey—the Garden State!

Did You Know?

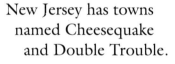

New Jersey was the first state to allow women to vote. The first state constitution granted women the vote in 1776. But New Jersey lawmakers took away that right in 1807. New Jersey women couldn't vote for more than 100 years after that.

Two of Thomas Edison's lesser-known inventions are wax paper and the talking doll.

Monopoly has sold more than 150 million copies in about twenty-three languages worldwide.

The medicine streptomycin has saved many lives. Selman Waksman discovered it in 1943. He was a research professor of microbiology at Rutgers University at the time. Waksman won a Nobel Prize for his work.

New Jersey has towns named Cheesequake and Double Trouble.

The Garden State also has towns named Blue Anchor, White Horse, Orange, Smoke Rise, Brick Town, and Ongs Hat.

In 1974, sixty-four-year-old Millicent Fenwick of Bernardsville was elected to the U.S. Congress. She was one of the first grandmothers to serve there. While in Congress (1975-1983), Fenwick fought for civil rights. She was related to John Stevens, who built the country's first locomotive when he was seventy-six.

Years ago, many people flew in airships rather than airplanes. Hydrogen was used to lift these cigar-shaped aircraft. The famous airship *Hindenburg* exploded at Lakehurst, New Jersey, on May 6, 1937. Thirty-six people were killed. This disaster ended the age of the airship for passenger service.

Long ago, a creature was said to have come out of the southern New Jersey swamps. People called it the New Jersey Devil. The creature had a horse's face. It had the body of a kangaroo and the wings of a bat. The strangest part was that the creature was friendly. New Jersey's hockey team was named for this legendary creature.

A road plan called a "cloverleaf" helps traffic flow safely on many highways. New Jersey had the country's first cloverleaf in 1929.

In 1933, the world's first drive-in movie theater opened outside Camden.

In 1881 near Atlantic City, James Lafferty, Jr., put up a six-story building in the shape of an elephant. Known as Lucy the Elephant, it is now a National Historic Landmark.

55

New Jersey Information

State flag

Purple violet

Eastern goldfinch

Area: 7,787 square miles (only four states are smaller)

Greatest Distance North to South: 167 miles

Greatest Distance East to West: 57 miles

Borders: New York to the north and northeast; the Atlantic Ocean to the east; Delaware Bay to the south; Delaware and Pennsylvania to the west

Highest Point: High Point, 1,803 feet above sea level

Lowest Point: Sea level, along the Atlantic Ocean

Hottest Recorded Temperature: 110° F. (at Runyon, on July 10, 1936)

Coldest Recorded Temperature: -34° F. (at River Vale, on January 5, 1904)

Statehood: The third state, on December 18, 1787

Origin of Name: New Jersey was named for England's Isle of Jersey

Capital: Trenton (since 1790)

Counties: 21

United States Senators: 2

United States Representatives: 13 (as of 1992)

State Senators: 40

State General Assembly Members: 80

State Motto: "Liberty and Prosperity"

Main Nickname: "Garden State"

Another Nickname: "Cockpit of the Revolution"

State Seal: Adopted in 1928

State Flag: Adopted in 1896

State Flower: Purple violet

State Bird: Eastern goldfinch

State Tree: Red oak

State Animal: Horse

State Dinosaur: Hadrasaurus

State Insect: Honeybee

Some Mountain Ranges: Kittatinny, Ramapo, Watchung

Some Rivers: Delaware, Hudson, Raritan, Hackensack, Passaic, Toms, Mullica, Great Egg Harbor, Maurice

Some Lakes: Lake Hopatcong, Lake Mohawk, and Budd, Culvers, Greenwood, and Swartswood lakes

Wildlife: Deer, foxes, raccoons, skunks, opossums, minks, otters, beavers, muskrats, turtles, whales, dolphins, seals, eastern goldfinches, sea gulls, ducks, geese, wild turkeys, ruffed grouse, partridges, pheasants

Manufactured Products: Chemicals (including medicines, soaps, and cleaners), foods, books, plastics, refined oil, glass, scientific instruments, jewelry, toys, sporting goods, office and art supplies, beverages, computers, tools, nails and other hardware, motor vehicles, electrical equipment, telephone equipment

Farm Products: Flowers, shrubs, milk, eggs, beef cattle, hogs, tomatoes, cabbage, lettuce, peaches, blueberries, cranberries

Mining Products: Crushed stone, sand and gravel, clay, peat

Fishing Products: Clams, lobsters, oysters, scallops, flounder, menhaden, sea bass

Population: 7,748,634, ninth among the fifty states (1990 U.S. Census Bureau figures)

Major Cities (1990 Census):

Newark	275,221
Jersey City	228,537
Paterson	140,891
Elizabeth	110,002
Edison	88,680
Trenton	88,675
Camden	87,492

Red oak

Opossum

Herring gull

New Jersey History

8,000 B.C.—Prehistoric Indians reach New Jersey

A.D. 1524—Giovanni da Verrazano explores New Jersey's coast for France

1609—Henry Hudson explores New Jersey's coast for the Netherlands

1638—Swedish settlers purchase land along Cape May from the Lenni-Lenape Indians

1660—The Dutch settle Bergen (now part of Jersey City), the first permanent non-Indian town in New Jersey

1664—England gains control of the New Jersey region

1666—Newark is settled

1746—Princeton University is begun

1766—Rutgers University is founded

1774—English tea is burned at the Greenwich Tea Party

1775-83—The Revolutionary War is fought

1776—The Americans win the Battle of Trenton on December 26

1777—The Americans win the Battle of Princeton on January 3

1778—The Battle of Monmouth is fought to a draw on June 28

1783—The United States wins the Revolutionary War

1787—New Jersey becomes the third state on December 18

1790—Trenton becomes the state capital

1791—Alexander Hamilton founds Paterson, the country's first planned industrial city

1809—John Stevens's *Phoenix* is the world's first steamboat to make a sea voyage

1824—Stevens builds the nation's first railroad locomotive

1838—Samuel F. B. Morse operates the country's first successful electric telegraph near Morristown

1858—The first dinosaur discovery in the country is made at Haddonfield

Thomas Edison's phonograph

1861-65—More than 88,000 New Jerseyans help the North win the Civil War

1879—Thomas Edison invents the electric light in Menlo Park

1884—Native New Jerseyan Grover Cleveland is elected the twenty-second president of the United States

1892—Grover Cleveland is elected the twenty-fourth president of the United States, becoming the only president to serve two terms that aren't back-to-back

1912—New Jersey's governor, Woodrow Wilson, is elected the twenty-eighth president of the United States

1917-18—After the United States enters World War I, about 130,000 New Jerseyans serve

1929-39—During the Great Depression, many New Jersey factories close, and huge numbers of people lose their jobs

1941-45—After the United States enters World War II, more than 560,000 New Jersey men and women serve

1952—The New Jersey Turnpike opens

1960—*Tiros I* is launched; it was developed in New Jersey

1962—*Telstar I* is launched; it, too, was developed in New Jersey

1967—A four-day riot in Newark ends with twenty-six deaths and over $10 million in damages

1969— Native New Jerseyan Edwin "Buzz" Aldrin becomes the second person to walk on the moon

1976—Gambling casinos are legalized for Atlantic City

1981—New Jerseyans vote to create a state fund for cleaning up toxic waste

1987—Happy 200th birthday, Garden State!

1989—James J. Florio is elected New Jersey's governor

1990—New Jersey's population reaches 7,748,634

1993—Liberty Science Center opens in Liberty State Park

The New Jersey Turnpike opened in 1952.

MAP KEY

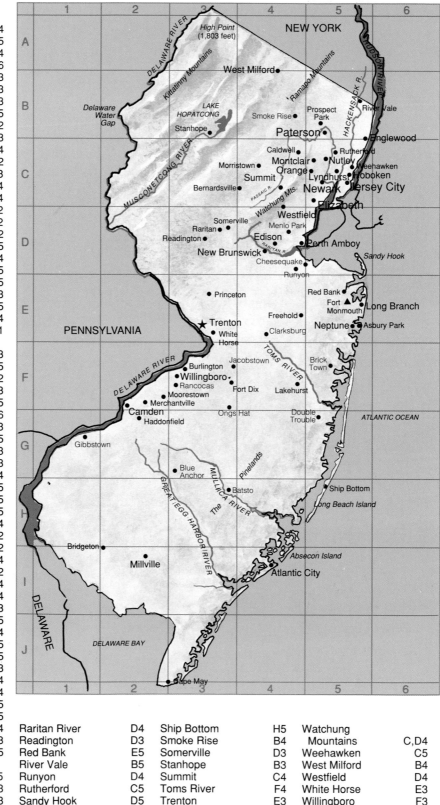

GLOSSARY

ancient: Relating to a time early in history

antislavery: Against slavery

astronaut: A person who is highly trained for spaceflight

capital: A city that is the seat of government

capitol: The building in which the government meets

casino: A room or building used for gambling

climate: The typical weather of a region

colony: A settlement that is outside a parent country and that is ruled by the parent country

constitution: A framework for government

dinosaur: Generally a huge animal that died out millions of years ago

duel: A kind of fight between two people to settle an argument

explorer: A person who visits and studies unknown lands

freedom: Being able to make one's own decisions

glacier: A mass of slowly moving ice

hurricane: A huge storm that forms over an ocean

industry: A business that uses many workers to make products

inventor: A person who comes up with a new machine or a new way of doing things

locomotive: An engine that pulls railroad cars

million: A thousand thousand (1,000,000)

permanent: Lasting

pollution: The harming of the environment

population: The number of people in a place

poverty: A lack of money

powwow: A gathering of American Indians

real estate business: The buying and selling of property

rebel: To fight against one's government

satellite: A machine that is launched into space to bring back information

sculptor: A person who makes statues and other three-dimensional artworks

slavery: A practice in which some people are owned by other people

tourism: The business of providing services such as food and lodging for travelers

wigwam: An American Indian home that is made of poles and covered by bark and other materials

INDEX

Page numbers in boldface type indicate illustrations.

ABOUT THE AUTHOR

Dennis Brindell Fradin is the author of 150 published children's books. His works for Childrens Press include the Young People's Stories of Our States series, the Disaster! series, and the Thirteen Colonies series. Dennis is married to Judith Bloom Fradin, who taught high-school and college English for many years. She is now Dennis's chief researcher. The Fradins are the parents of two sons, Anthony and Michael, and a daughter, Diana. Dennis graduated from Northwestern University in 1967 with a B.A. in creative writing, and has lived in Evanston, Illinois, since that year.